SUPER BOWL

NEW YORK GIANTS

CHAMPIONS

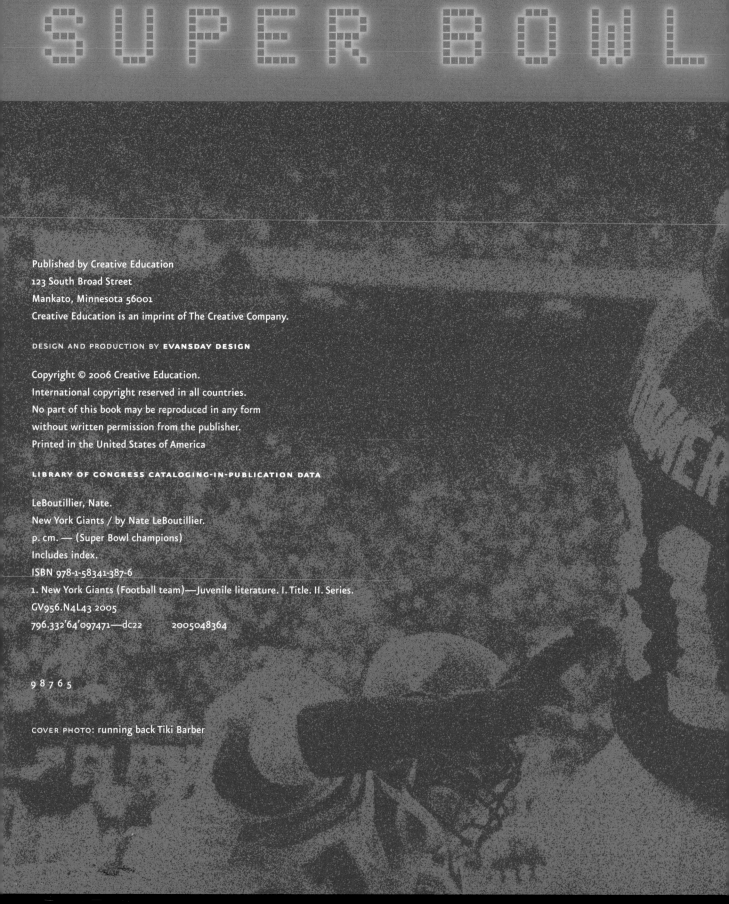

SUPER BOWL

Published by Creative Education

123 South Broad Street

Mankato, Minnesota 56001

Creative Education is an imprint of The Creative Company.

DESIGN AND PRODUCTION BY **EVANSDAY DESIGN**

LIBRARY OF CONGRESS CATALOGING-IN-PUBLICATION DATA

LeBoutillier, Nate.

New York Giants / by Nate LeBoutillier.

p. cm. — (Super Bowl champions)

Includes index.

ISBN 978-1-58341-387-6

1. New York Giants (Football team)—Juvenile literature. I. Title. II. Series.

GV956.N4L43 2005

796.332′64′097471—dc22   2005048364

9 8 7 6 5

COVER PHOTO: running back Tiki Barber

PHOTOGRAPHS BY

AP/Wide World Photos, Corbis (Bettmann, Michael Kim), Getty Images (Al Bello, Steve Dykes/Allsport, T.G. Higgins, Paul Spinelli), SportsChrome USA

THE GIANTS are a professional football team in the National Football League (NFL). They play in East Rutherford, New Jersey. The weather can be cold when the Giants play.

THE GIANTS play in a stadium called Giants Stadium. Their helmets are blue with the letters "NY" on the side. Their uniforms are blue, red, and white. The Giants play many games against teams called the Cowboys, Eagles, and Redskins.

THE GIANTS played their first season in 1925. The team's owner was named Tim Mara. He bought the team for just $500. In 1927, the Giants won their first NFL championship. That made them world champions. They were champions again in 1934 and 1938.

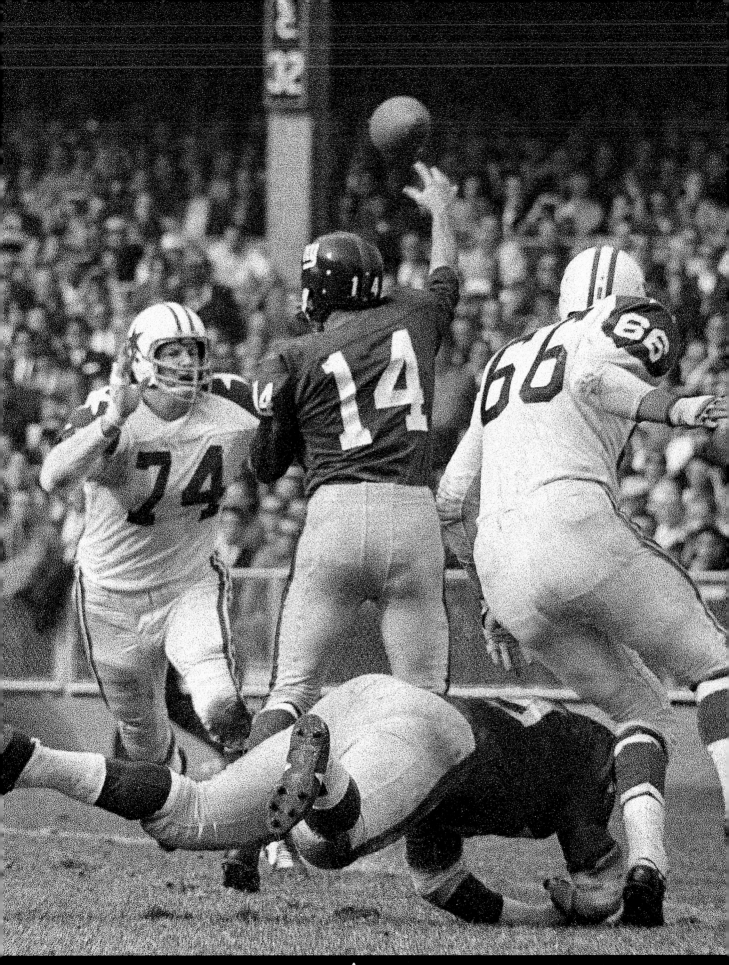

IN 1958, the Giants played the Baltimore Colts in a famous game. Some people call it "The Greatest Game Ever Played." Fifteen players who would get into the Hall of Fame played in the game. Lots of fans watched the game on TV. But the Giants lost.

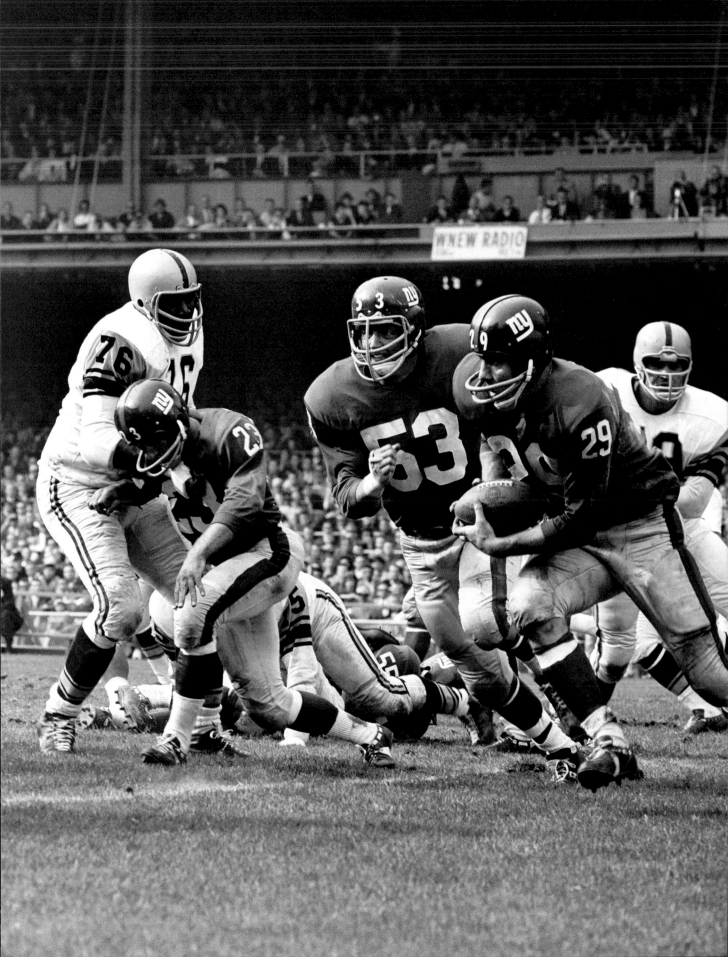

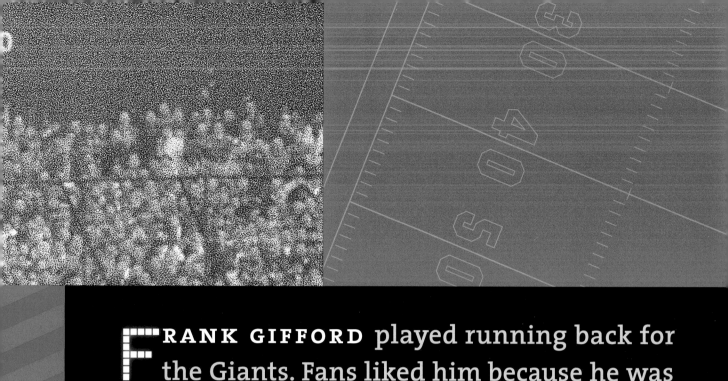

FRANK GIFFORD played running back for the Giants. Fans liked him because he was fast and good-looking. He helped the team win another NFL championship in 1956.

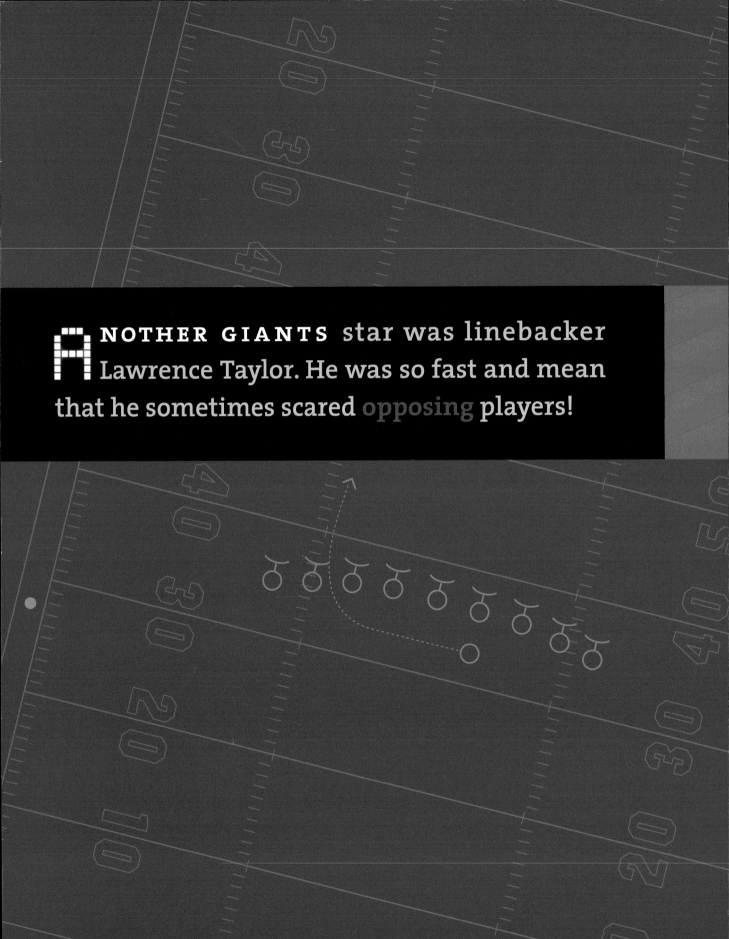

ANOTHER GIANTS star was linebacker Lawrence Taylor. He was so fast and mean that he sometimes scared opposing players!

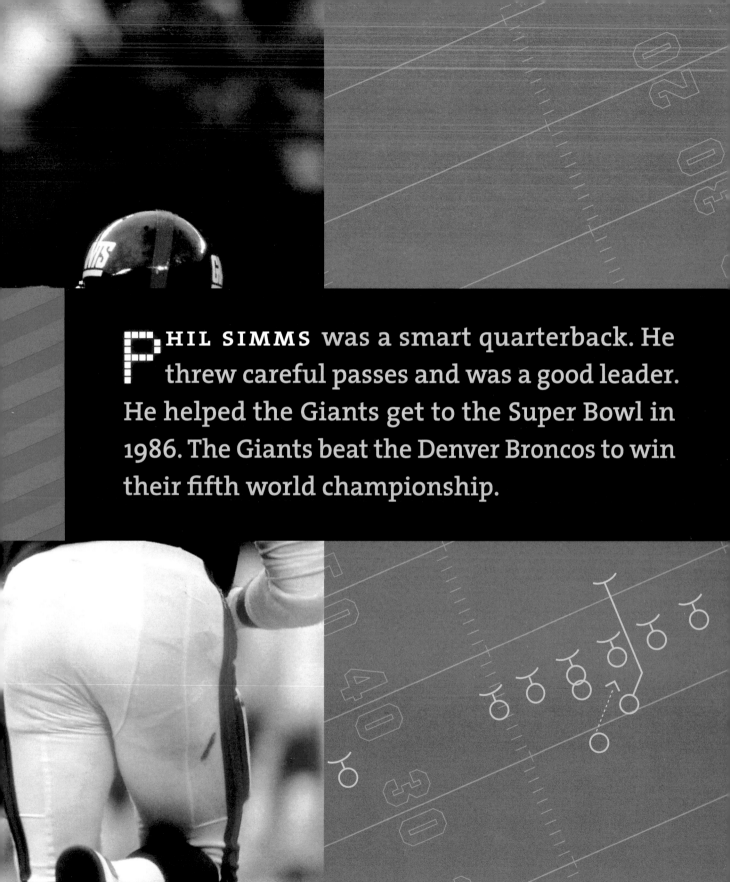

PHIL SIMMS was a smart quarterback. He threw careful passes and was a good leader. He helped the Giants get to the Super Bowl in 1986. The Giants beat the Denver Broncos to win their fifth world championship.

THE **GIANTS** won another Super Bowl in 1990. They played the Buffalo Bills in an exciting game. The Bills' kicker missed a kick at the end of the game, and the Giants won 20–19.

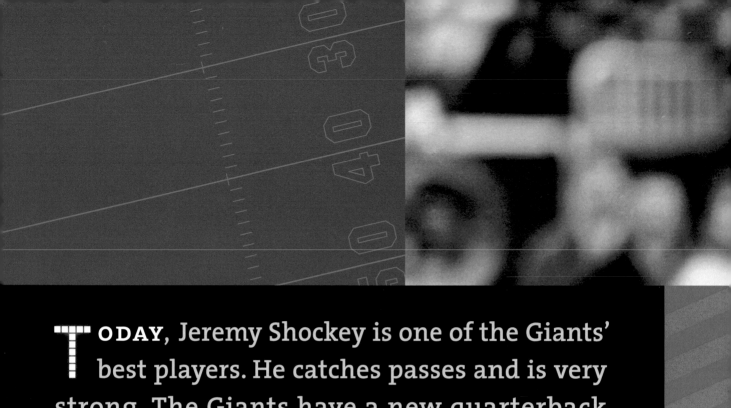

TODAY, Jeremy Shockey is one of the Giants' best players. He catches passes and is very strong. The Giants have a new quarterback named Eli Manning, too. Giants fans hope that these players will help the team win another Super Bowl!

GLOSSARY

Hall of Fame

a club that only the best NFL players and coaches
get to join

National Football League (NFL)

a group of football teams that play against each other;
there are 32 teams in the NFL today

opposing

on the other team or side

professional

a person or team that gets paid to play or work

Team colors
Blue, red, and white

Home stadium
Giants Stadium (80,242 seats)

Conference/Division
National Football Conference (NFC), East Division

First season
1925

Super Bowl wins
1986 (beat Denver Broncos 39–20)
1990 (beat Buffalo Bills 20–19)

Training camp location
Albany, New York

Giants Web site for kids
http://giants.com/fan_zone/Youth.asp

NFL Web site for kids
http://www.playfootball.com